HOW THE
GOSPEL
MOVES FROM
FRIEND
TO
FRIEND

Published by Advance
3 London Road, Redhill, RH1 1LY, United Kingdom,
www.advancemovement.com

ISBN 978-1-9163691-4-6 (paperback)
ISBN 978-1-9163691-5-3 (e-book)

All italicizations in scripture passages have been added by the author.
A catalogue record of this book is available from the British Library.

Cover Design by Nathan Lambert
Typeset in Adobe Garamond Pro and Brandon Grotesque

HOW THE GOSPEL MOVES FROM FRIEND TO FRIEND

BY PJ SMYTH

Published by **Advance**

OTHER BOOKS BY PJ SMYTH

Crossing the Line of Faith

A short book for churches to give to people who are considering crossing the line of faith, or who recently have.

Through the Waters of Baptism

A short book for churches to give to people who are considering getting baptized, or who recently have.

Elders

A book to train potential elders and revitalize existing elders.

CONTENTS

HOW TO USE THIS BOOK

You can read this book **by yourself** or with a **group of believers**.

If you are reading it as a group, before you meet each read the chapter(s) and answer the reflection questions individually. When you gather you can use these answers as the basis for discussion. Or, because the material is concise, you could read the material together when you meet and then plunge straight into discussion using the *Reflection and discussion* sections as a guide.

How the Gospel Moves from Friend to Friend

THE GLORIOUS GOSPEL

We must surely start our short journey together through the pages ahead by celebrating the glorious gospel. Before learning to pass it on to our friends, let us receive it again ourselves under three simple headings: *Jesus and grace*, *Saved and changed*, and *First and full*.

JESUS AND GRACE

The gospel is a person, the God-Man Jesus Christ the Son of God (Mk. 1:1, Rom. 1:9). Jesus, and therefore the gospel, is characterized by grace. So central is grace to Jesus that the Apostle Paul even personified Jesus as grace, and so central is grace to the gospel that Paul called it the "gospel of grace" (Titus 2:11, Acts 20:24). In our merit-based world, people are used to getting what they deserve. But the grace-based gospel gives people what they don't deserve. We could say that *the gospel is the good news of how God graciously interacts with humanity through Jesus.*

SAVED AND CHANGED

Titus 2:11 tells us that Jesus (the gospel) both saves us and trains us to live in a godly manner. We could say that *the gospel saves me in a moment, and changes me over time. It delivers me from the penalty of sin in a moment, and from the power of sin over time.*

We are **saved** by grace through faith. This means that we access God's grace simply through belief. Actually, even the ability to believe is a gracious gift from God (Eph. 2:8-10). The Bible teaches that all have sinned, and that before a holy God the penalty for sin is death (Rom. 3:23, 6:23). God's justice demands the penalty of death be exacted, but God's love caused Jesus to come and die as a substitute in our place. It is the gracious exchange: the sinless One takes on our sin, that we sinners can take on his righteousness (2 Cor. 5:21). Gratefully believing in this is what it means to be saved by grace through faith.

Once we are saved, the astounding reality of Jesus dying in our place continues to work in us to increasingly **change** us to live godly and joyful lives. *God dying for me* is a supernaturally endowed truth, and applying it to different areas of our lives effects genuine change. For example, when Paul tells husbands to love their wives, he says they should do so "as Christ loved the church" (Eph. 5:25). He is telling husbands to think deeply about the glorious way that Jesus loved them by dying for them, and then love their wives out of that reserve of gratitude. Space doesn't permit elaboration on more examples, but the same applies to giving money (2 Cor. 8:7-9), forgiving others (Matt. 18:22-35), and refraining from anxiety (Rom. 8:32).

FIRST AND FULL

In terms of the gospel, the Apostle Paul considered a basic understanding of the cross of Jesus to be of "**first** importance" (1 Cor. 15:1-4). However, Paul also spoke of the gospel in terms of the "**full** counsel of God" (Acts 20:25-27). This means that although the cross is the epicenter of the gospel, there are other truths flowing to and from the cross that are also part of the counsel of gospel truth.

If we abbreviate our gospel definition to no more than the cross per se (i.e. how the substitutionary death of Jesus gives *me* eternal life), we run the risk of producing abbreviated believers who understate how the cross presses us into Christian community and mission. We also limit the options unbelievers have in terms of *approaching* the cross. They must end up face to face with the stark truths of the cross, but they are often helped in getting there by one of the avenues to the cross found in the full gospel.

We will talk about *helpful* ways to present unbelievers with *first* and *full* elements of the gospel at the end of the book in *Gospel communication*. As most readers will be clearer on what I mean by "first" than "full", I will take a moment here to briefly outline just four meta-themes of the full gospel:

*The gospel is that through Jesus God is **renewing all things**, and by faith I can be part of that renewal.* Early in Genesis, the advent of sin turned a new world old. Late in Revelation, the second advent of Christ turns the old world new (Rev. 21:5). Between these two poles Jesus came to earth to *start* the process of renewal. He made blind eyes see, and sick bodies well. He brought peace in lieu of strife. And, wonderfully, within this greater theme of cosmic renewal, he offers personal renewal to people (Jn. 3:3, 2 Cor. 5:17-18).

But understanding my *personal* renewal within the context of *cosmic* renewal is very important. Not only does it protect me from a me-and-Jesus gospel diminution, but it makes my salvation *robust*: despite temporary trials, I know I have a trial-free eternity awaiting me (Rom. 8:18)!

*The gospel is that through Jesus the gracious rule of **God's kingdom** is advancing across the earth, and by faith I can be a citizen of that kingdom.* The Bible also speaks of the "gospel of the kingdom" (Matt. 4:23). The kingdom of God is wherever God's rule is. When Christ returns, God's kingdom will be comprehensively established. But when Jesus came to earth, he began the advance of God's kingdom. He brought the values and characteristics of heaven to earth (healing, peace, joy) and he charges his followers to pray and live in a way that brings the kingdom to earth (Matt. 6:10, Mk. 16:17-18).

Understanding my personal citizenship within the wider context of God's kingdom is very important. The concept of citizenship eliminates any possibility of me thinking I can follow Jesus outside of *Christian community*. Jesus taught us to pray "Our Father" – a big clue right there. A kingdom mindset also underlines the element of *obedience and repentance* – Jesus is not only my savior but my king, and therefore he gets to define right and wrong, not I. Furthermore, it adds a radical edge to my followership of Jesus – remember, the kingdom of God is like a man who found treasure in a field and went and sold *all he had* to buy the field (Matt. 13:44). And, it gives me great *confidence*: the kingdom of God is like a small seed that will certainly grow into a huge tree (Matt. 13:31-32).

*The gospel is that through Jesus God is **gathering a people**, and by faith I can be a part of that people.* God has always wanted a people. The Bible begins with sweet harmony between God and Adam and Eve, and ends with multitudes around God's throne. And in between came Jesus to make a way for these multitudes to come to God. He tore the curtain. Branches can now be grafted into

Christ. Once we were not a people, but now through Christ we are a people (1 Pet. 2:10).

Once again, locating myself within the wider gospel theme of a gathered people decimates a reductionist "just-me-and-Jesus" gospel. The gospel is first *collective* (God wants a people), and secondly *personal* (I get to be part of that people).

*The gospel is that through Jesus **God's spirit** is filling the earth, and I can personally be filled with his spirit.* As a result of man's sin, in the Old Testament God's Spirit was mostly restricted to *places* such as Mount Sinai, the Ark of the Covenant, the Tabernacle, and the Temple. Although some key *people* experienced God's indwelling Spirit, the norm was that God's presence was found in *places not people.* But when Jesus came, this got reversed and *people* were filled with the Spirit (Lk. 3:16, Jn. 7:37-39, Acts 2:1-4, 16-18). The construction of the new Temple had begun, a temple of *people*, of living stones (Eph. 2:22, 1 Pet. 2:5). And the gospel story climaxes with God's presence being as all-encompassing as light (Rev. 22:5).

Locating myself within this great gospel theme helps me understand that being filled with the Spirit is not an optional extra, but a fundamental characteristic of God's people.

All made possible by the cross, these four meta-themes help us celebrate a gloriously full gospel of not only being saved by Jesus through the cross, but through the cross being part of a new world, a new kingdom, a new people, and empowered by God's Spirit.

REFLECTION AND DISCUSSION

In your own words, what do you understand by "first" and "full"?

Which of the four "full" gospel truths most causes your heart to be warmed, and why?

PART 1

GET
MOTIVATED

How the Gospel Moves from Friend to Friend

1
PRACTICAL REASONS
FOR FRIEND-TO-FRIEND

WESTERN CULTURE

Many people I know crossed the line of faith after hearing the gospel *preached publicly* or *passed on personally* by a friend. However, in the West public preaching alone – without the friend-to-friend dynamic – does not seem to "cut it." A friend-to-friend approach is needed more than ever for the following reasons.

First, due to an increasingly secular worldview, most unbelievers have a **minimal grasp on the basics** of the Christian faith. This means they are unlikely to understand and believe the gospel through a one-off sermon or conversation. Instead, they will probably need multiple encounters with the gospel, something best achieved through a steady friendship with a believer.

Second, the Western appreciation for *logic* combined with the cultural drift to *relativism* (no absolute truth) means that unbelievers usually have significant **presuppositional objections** to Christianity such as "the Bible is full of errors" or "how can a loving God let bad things happen?" Until these objections are partially addressed, they may be unwilling to consider Christianity. But their questions can be addressed over time through a friendship with a believer who discusses the issues with them, passes them helpful resources, or introduces them to a Christian with more knowledge or training in this area.

Third, many Westerners are increasingly resistant to Christianity due to the **unhelpful stereotypes** of Christians propagated on social media. The social media revolution has given a voice to people with extreme views and agendas, including some polarizing Christians who judge much and love little. When our church surveyed our unchurched friends on their top gripes with Christianity, they were not the huge philosophical challenges of the apparent unfairness of hell or the exclusive nature of the claims of Christ, they were "Christians are hypocritical and judgmental!" Fortunately, such intolerant caricatures can be dispelled through a friendship with a Christian.

Fourth, many unbelievers today **wrongly assume they are Christians** when they are not. Some have grown up in cultures where "everyone" is considered Catholic from birth, or have been raised in the "Bible Belt" where American citizenship and Christian faith are seen as one and the same. Such people often assume they are accepted by God as a kind of birthright. Because of this extremely powerful delusion, many of them do not feel the need to engage with church, or if they do, they are inoculated against genuine faith. These religious conservatives might be the hardest group to reach with the gospel. They desperately need friendships with authentic Christians to help them into saving faith in Jesus.

CHURCH EFFECTIVENESS

Sunday church meetings, Easter productions, Alpha courses and the like can only be evangelistically fruitful if unbelievers actually attend (!) and they usually only attend when a trusted **Christian friend invites them**. After the meeting they will likely need to keep talking about the claims and teachings of Christ too, something they will need a Christian friend for.

Also, when people cross the line of faith, **healthy integration into a church** is more likely if they have a trusted friend who is already part of that church community. Joining a brand new community of people with new beliefs and practices can be daunting, and a pre-existing friendship will be a great help.

LESS RISKY, MORE FRUITFUL

Finally, friend-to-friend evangelism is generally less risky and more fruitful than stranger-to-stranger evangelism. Stranger-to-stranger evangelism refers to things like striking up conversations with people next to you on the plane or in line with you at the store, or even "cold calling" door to door. In the short time you have with them, you try to share some aspect of the gospel with them such as, "*I don't know you, but I know that God does, and he loves you. And, he sent Jesus to die in your place so that you can have eternal life. Do you know that?*" Or, you might be less direct by offering to pray for a challenge in their life that they have just been telling you about. All of us should be ready for this kind of engagement (with *Your story*, and *Gospel communication*, which we will look at in later chapters), and some believers are uniquely skilled at it. Sometimes stranger-to-stranger seems to bear immediate fruit; other times we have to trust it is good seed sown. However, stranger-to-stranger is hard to do well, and if done badly it can cause the person to step *away* from the line of faith.

However, many of the risks of offending the stranger are reduced by the friend-to-friend approach. When you have some knowledge of the person, you can frame the gospel in a way that is most helpful to their unique disposition and situation. If you are their friend, you will be less inclined to "Bible bash" them because you will have to see them again in a few days' time! And if you have already proven that you genuinely see them as your friend rather than an evangelistic project, they will be less suspicious of your motives when you do start to engage with them on spiritual things.

REFLECTION AND DISCUSSION

With which of these practical reasons for friend-to-friend do you most resonate, and why?

Can you think of other pragmatic arguments for friend-to-friend?

2
BIBLICAL REASONS
FOR FRIEND-TO-FRIEND

It should be impossible to read the Bible without acknowledging the primacy of mission to the Christian faith. *Generally* speaking, mission refers to an outward-oriented posture that works to improve society by caring for the poor and standing for social justice. Often such general humanitarian endeavors are done without any agenda to make converts. More *specifically*, mission refers to direct evangelistic efforts to help people become Christians. Both aspects of mission are essential to fulfilling Christ's command to love our neighbors. With this dual definition of mission in mind, let's look at the missional nature of *God*, the missional call on *the Church*, and the pattern of friend-to-friend evangelism for *individual believers*.

MISSIONAL GOD

At the heart of God's very nature is evangelism. The Father sent the Son to earth to preach the gospel (Jn. 3:17, 20:21). The Father and the Son sent the Spirit to earth as a gospel agent to convict the world about sin, righteousness and judgement (Jn. 14:26, 15:26, 16:8-11). Now the Son sends us to neighborhoods and nations to preach the gospel (Matt. 28:18-20, Mk. 1:17, Jn. 13:20, Acts 1:8).

The work of the Spirit in God's people is multifaceted. One key aspect of his work is to empower us for mission. He anointed

Jesus for mission (Lk. 4:16-21) and he anointed the disciples for mission (Jn. 20:21-23, Acts 1:8), something he still does for Christ-followers today.

Jesus embodied mission by being Immanuel, "God with us." He introduced his ministry by reading a passage from Isaiah with the clearest possible statement of missional intent (see Lk. 4:18-21). That text set the trajectory for three years of evangelism to crowds and individuals through words and works. George McLeod contends:

> I simply argue that the cross be raised again at the center of the market place, as well as on the steeple of the church. Jesus was not crucified in a Cathedral between two candles, but on a cross between two thieves, on a town garbage heap at a crossroads of politics so cosmopolitan they had to write His title in Hebrew and Latin and Greek. And the kind of place where cynics talk smut and thieves curse and soldiers gamble. Because that is where He died and that is what He died about. And that is where Christ's people ought to be and what church people ought to be about.[1]

Let's turn now to what "church people ought to be about."

MISSIONAL CHURCH

At the **inauguration of God's people** in the Old Testament, God said to Abram, "I will make of you a great nation, and I will bless you and make your name great, so that you will be a blessing...

16

and in you all the families of the earth shall be blessed" (Gen. 12:1-3). God's original purpose in having a blessed people of his own was so he could *bless the nations of the world through them.* Evangelism is not an add-on. It is not an optional extra. It is the core of who we are. Right from the start we were designed to be an outward-looking, other-oriented, mission-driven, soul-winning, evangelistic people.

In the New Testament, Jesus issued an updated version of the Abrahamic commission that we call the **Great Commission** (Matt. 28:18-20, Acts 1:8). In these last words before his return to heaven, Jesus could have prioritized any number of things, but he told us to go and preach the gospel. Just before I left the house last week I told my sons to tidy their rooms. They didn't say, "Interesting idea, Dad. We will form a committee to discuss the feasibility of your proposal." They simply obeyed my commission to tidy their rooms. The Great Commission is to be obeyed not discussed.

The **early church** as a whole obeyed Jesus' commission to get on mission. They filled Jerusalem with the gospel (Acts 5:28) and caused a civil uproar (Acts 21:30-31). They became so prominent in Antioch that they were given the name Christians (Acts 11:26). Their commitment to evangelism divided cities (Acts 14:4), threatened municipal economies (Acts 19:23-41), and "caused trouble all over the world" (Acts 17:6). Because of their fervor new believers were added to their number daily (Acts 2:47).

Early church leaders personally led the way in evangelism. Peter actively participated in various one-to-one evangelistic encounters and led a revival in Jerusalem that saw thousands cross the line of faith (Acts 2:14-3:10). Philip had an extraordinary run of evangelistic activity in Acts 8. He preached to the citizens of Samaria, baptized an Ethiopian politician on the road to Gaza, and then continued through Azotus to Caesarea. And Paul, despite his resolve to help disciples mature in Christ (Col. 1:28), said his primary ambition was calling unbelievers to faith and preaching the gospel "where Christ was not known" (Rom. 1:5, Rom 15:20 NIV). "I have become all things to all people," he said, "that by all means I might save some" (1 Cor. 9:22).

Why was the early church so devoted to mission? Because they believed **Jesus' missional metaphors** of the Church. He called us to be *salt*, bringing much-needed kingdom flavor to our neighbors, widows, orphans, the oppressed, the depressed, and the spiritually blind. When salt stays in the salt shaker, not only does the "meat" of society rot, but so does the salt! Without the priority of evangelistic mission, life in the salt shaker becomes stifling and petty. In a vain attempt to keep church life stimulating, the grains of salt begin to squabble about minutia. Before long the church becomes unhappy, marginalized, tasteless, and irrelevant to society.

Jesus also called us to be *light*, not hidden in our sanctuaries but giving light to our cities. We have good news to herald not hoard. And he called us to be yeast, a baking substance that is designed to spread through the dough, not remain in its tin. Rather than choosing between church or society, we are supposed to be church *through* society. We are an infiltration agency, not an evacuation agency. Christopher Wright concludes:

> It is not so much the case that God has a mission for his church in the world, as that God has a church for his mission in the world. Mission was not made

for the church; the church was made for mission—God's mission.[2]

MISSIONAL ME

When Jesus recruited the first disciples, he said to them, "Follow me, and I will make you become fishers of men" (Mk. 1:17). Interesting. He called them to follow him and then, in the same breath, he called them to *call others* to follow him. Similarly, Jesus told another brand new convert, "Go home to your friends and tell them how much the Lord has done for you, and how he has had mercy on you" (Mk. 5:19). In both instances Jesus clearly considered personal evangelism an integral part of following him.

In John 1:35-51 there is a brilliant sequence of friend-to-friend activity. It starts when Andrew and a friend overhear John the Baptist say that Jesus is the Messiah. This piques their interest and they have a brief conversation with Jesus. Then Andrew goes and gets his brother, Simon Peter, and introduces him to Jesus. The next day, Philip becomes a Christ-follower and immediately tells his friend Nathanael about Jesus. Nathanael is skeptical at first, but Philip persuades him to "come and see" for himself who Jesus is. He does, and he too becomes a follower of Christ!

Can you see the **pattern of friend-to-friend** evangelism emerging? Don Carson writes:

> This has been the foundational principle of Christian expansion ever since: new followers of Jesus bear witness of him to others, who in turn become disciples and repeat the process.[3]

Paul makes the same point in 2 Corinthians 5:17-20, affirming that *anyone* who is in Christ is reconciled to God and that *all* believers now have the ministry of helping reconcile others to God.

The pattern continues in the **Book of Acts**. In Acts 8 we learn that those who were scattered from Jerusalem shared the gospel (Acts 8:1-4). Sometimes the gospel was shared with a complete stranger (e.g. Philip with the Ethiopian politician), but more commonly it was shared on the back of a preexisting friendship. For example, Epaphras shared the gospel with the Colossians through friendship (Col. 1:7). Paul shared it with the Thessalonians through friendship (1 Thess. 2:7-8). Similarly, Cornelius' conversion caused his whole household to come to faith (Acts 10) as did the conversions of Lydia and the Philippian jailor (Acts 16). In those days "household" (Greek *oikos*) referred to an entire social network of immediate and extended family, servants and their families, business associates and neighbors. Clearly, the gospel must have spread friend-to-friend through these social networks.

God calls every single believer, not just pastors and evangelists, to faithfully share the gospel with others. Every member of Christ's body is a missionary.

REFLECTION AND DISCUSSION

Which of the three sections (Missional God, Missional Church, and Missional me) has most impacted you, and why?

Was there a particular truth in one of the sections that grabbed your attention?

3
MISSION POSSIBLE

Although biblically convinced about the missional responsibility of God, the Church and every believer, it can be daunting to actually take *personal* responsibility for evangelism. Maybe the shadow of certain failure is already starting to creep up on you: *Why haven't you been better at this before? How are you going to get going in friend-to-friend evangelism, let alone sustain it?* Here are some thoughts to help counter any condemning and confusing thoughts in this vein, and encourage you that friend-to-friend is possible for you.

THINK POWER AND GRACE

Since the moment Adam and Eve sinned, God has been on an unrelenting mission to "seek and to save the lost" (Lk. 19:10). Don't feel that your friendship with your unbelieving friend is impotent. God *himself* is making *his* appeal to unbelievers through you (2 Cor. 5:20). You're the pipe and he's the **power**. That's a strong team. Only God can save people—not you. Ultimately, no one can profess that Jesus is Lord except by the Holy Spirit (1 Cor. 12:3). The Spirit's power is more important than our wise and persuasive words or actions (1 Cor. 2:4-5). So be purposeful but not driven.

In terms of **grace**, I recently asked a college student how she was feeling about her upcoming exam. She replied, "Pretty good. I can blow it and still pass the course!" Listen, you can blow the friend-to-friend mission of evangelism and God will still love, accept, and delight in you as much as if you were the world's greatest evangelist. Isn't that wonderful? Isn't that freeing?

THINK STEPS

Imagine a line painted on the ground. Think of crossing that line as crossing the line of faith, or conversion. Most people take many steps over time before they reach the line of faith. Necessary steps often include having positive experiences with individual Christians and churches, having some questions answered, and of course actually understanding hearing a clear presentation of the gospel. (Actually, research suggests that unbelievers need to hear the gospel explained six times before it sticks). Of course, having a good Christian friend is not only a key step in itself, but also something that helps the person take other steps.

Therefore, the definition of evangelistic success should be "did they take a step, or even half a step, closer to the line of faith?" rather than "did they cross the line of faith?" Defining success in this way means all of us can play a significant part in someone's journey toward the line of faith. Even seemingly insignificant words or actions can be a key step in someone's journey to faith. I have a friend who selflessly gave a bottle of water to someone he barely knew who was dehydrated. By chance they saw each other a year later, and the man told my friend that his act of kindness was a significant moment in his journey to God.

THINK FRIENDSHIP, CREWS, AND TOOLS

The remainder of the book is about leveraging these things for gospel advance. By way of introduction, if "evangelism" sounds too scary to you, think "**friendship**" instead. If you form a good friendship with an unbeliever you will inevitably influence them toward faith because good friends talk about things that are meaningful to them.

If the prospect of working alone sounds scary to you, then join a "**crew**." In Jesus' era, fishermen worked together in teams using large nets, so when Jesus called his disciples to fish for men, he likely had fishing crews in mind rather than a lone fisherman casting his line into a remote mountain stream. Crews are groups of believers who fish together, and they are more effective and fun than fishing alone.

If the thought of initiating a conversation about Christian things – or explaining Christian truths – makes you apprehensive, having a few **tools** in your friend-to-friend toolbox can be great help with that. We will look at some of these tools in Chapter 6.

REFLECTION AND DISCUSSION

Which of these perspectives particularly encourage you that friend-to-friend is possible, and why?

How the Gospel Moves from Friend to Friend

PART 2

GET
GOING

4
FRIENDSHIP

Some people are friend magnets, having more non-Christian friends than they know what to do with. But most of us need some encouragement and ideas to make friends with unbelievers. Here are some suggestions of how to *make friends*, *be a good friend*, and *naturally engage on spiritual things*.

MAKE FRIENDS

First, **pick** a few unbelievers or prodigals you will try to befriend, or with whom you will try to deepen an existing friendship. Think of this group as your priority group. It will change over time, and along the way don't neglect others. But if you shoot at nothing, that is exactly what you will hit! As you consider which friendships to prioritize, think about the different *social networks* that you may already be part of, such as *family*, *neighbors*, *colleagues*, and those with *shared interests*.

Second, start to **pray** for this group. Prayer is our secret weapon. It is oil on the rusty hinges of an unbeliever's heart. It is gentle rain on the hard soil of their soul. Pray that the Lord would open their minds to understand the gospel, and that God would use you as his ambassador to make his appeal through you (2 Cor. 5:20). As any true friend would, also pray for the various issues in their lives and the challenges that they are facing.

Third, **prioritize** time with this group. Life is busy, so instead of making it busier, rather leverage your current activities and rhythms of life for maximum evangelistic impact. Of course, you may need to make some adjustments to how you spend your time, but usually just being more intentional *within* our existing rhythms of life can lead to effective friend-to-friend. Think about how you could do this in the following areas of life:

Work: How could you capitalize on relational opportunities with coworkers? Lunch hour? Office parties? Being generally more emotionally engaged and proactive in friendship building?

School students: Could you join a study group rather than working alone? Could you join a club or society to meet people with similar interests?

School parents: Could you invite your children's friends over for a meal? Could you invite the families from the class or team over for a cookout?

Gym: Could you join a class rather than working out alone?

Hobbies: Could you switch from running alone to running with a club? Could you join or start a book club? Golf club? Chess club? Gaming group? Toddler's group?

TV: Do you have friends who are "groupies" of a TV show, or a sports team? Could you join them to watch the games/shows?

Neighborhood gatherings: Could you initiate a block party, or a weekly activity for the neighborhood kids?

Meals: Could you carve out one meal a week when you always eat with someone who doesn't know Jesus?

BE A GOOD FRIEND

To build and deepen friendships, you need to **put in the time**. Eating together is great for consolidating friendship. I have also found that friendships forge fast when you do things that your friend enjoys. A friend of mine had a passion for tennis. When I became his doubles partner, our friendship leapt forward and he crossed the line of faith a couple of months later, while we were chatting after a tennis match.

I ask my friends **lots of questions**. I ask for their views on politics, religion, sports, and current affairs. As trust grows over time, I ask them what they find hardest in their job, marriage, and life. I also ask what satisfies them. Because only Jesus ultimately satisfies, this often leads to deeper conversation about faith.

In John 4, when Jesus asked the woman at the well for water, he was being **vulnerable**. This is an important aspect of friendship. Don't think that you always need to be the "strong one." Ask for your friend's help and advice. Share your struggles. This can be as simple as asking a neighbor to lend you a drill and coach you on repairing your deck. Or it can be much deeper. When I had cancer, I expressed my doubts and fears to some of my unsaved friends, and I genuinely appreciated their wisdom and support in certain areas. When my unsaved friend says, "Man, parenting teenagers is hard," I may say something like, "Yeah. I am still trying to figure it out also. Give me your best tip."

In addition to receiving their care, welcome the different opportunities you will have to **care for them**. A simple text message or call may be a significant source of emotional support during exams, a tough stretch at work, or a relational break-up. Maybe you could offer more practical help, like dropping off a meal or lending them your car when theirs is in the shop.

We witness by both connecting and contrasting. We need to be **different but not holier-than-thou**. For example, you might stay at the office staff party for a couple of hours, but pull out when the party moves on to a strip club. These moments of contrast might feel awkward but they are an important part of pleasing Jesus and being a good witness, *and* they will likely lead to opportunities to talk about spiritual things. The segue might be someone making a joke about you being a goody-goody, but at least it's a segue! God will give you wisdom to respond without being defensive or judgmental.

Finally, remember there is a reason they call it fishing not catching. **Stay the course**. As my friend Donnie Griggs says, "You sure ain't gonna catch fish sitting at home alone watching Netflix." Maybe your unsaved friends need time to see if you and your faith are genuine. Be a faithful friend and guard your credibility for when the moment is right.

NATURALLY ENGAGE ON SPIRITUAL THINGS

If you are being a reasonable friend, opportunities to talk about spiritual things will naturally present themselves. However, to nudge things along I recommend the following:

Let them know that you are a Christian in a natural, unforced way. I usually do this *indirectly* by weaving into a conversation that I "had Bible Study last night" or that "I went to a great restaurant after church on Sunday." Or, I do it more directly by saying something like, "Church is a big part of my life" or "a friend of mine recently died in a car crash, which is testing my faith."

Ask if they are interested in spiritual things. In a relaxed and conversational manner, I might say, "Do you have any experience with spiritual things?" or "Are you a person of faith?" or "Do you do church at all?" Depending on their response, I either back off and live to fight another day or I follow up with something like, "Interesting. Tell me more about that." But no matter what they say, I do not show disapproval. I am genuinely interested in hearing their view of faith and want to understand them better. Remember, I am their friend.

Look for opportunities to talk more deeply about spiritual things. Depending on your personality, this may be easy or awkward. I am a reasonably strong conversationalist, so I like steering the conversation toward spiritual or philosophical topics. For example, if my friend and I are talking politics, I might ask if he thinks politics has become a substitute for religion and see where that leads. Or, if we are talking about the recent death of a celebrity, I might say, "Yeah, death is big deal. Do you think much about the afterlife? What do you think happens?"

Invite them to church. The number one reason people say they don't go to church is because no one has ever invited them! You might say something like, "I would love to see what you make of our church, would you like to come this Sunday?" Or, "Our friend Beth is getting baptized and I reckon we should support her. You up for that?" Or, "Our church is doing something special for Moms on Mother's Day. Why don't we both bring our Moms along then treat them to lunch afterwards?"

Keep your tools sharp. Later in the book we look at three important tools in your friend-to-friend toolbox. The first is *your story*, a 30-second vignette of how you became a Christian. The second is a *read-and-discuss* resource to provide a conversational yet structured context for you to talk about spiritual things with your friend. The third is *Gospel communication*, a way to concisely communicate the saving message of the cross of Jesus.

REFLECTION AND DISCUSSION

Write down the names of some unbelievers or prodigals from your various social networks (family, neighbors, colleagues, shared interests).

What steps could you take to better leverage your existing rhythms of life for friend-to-friend?

Are there any new rhythms or activities you could introduce to help with friend-to-friend?

Which of the suggestions about being a good friend most resonate with you, and why?

Which of the suggestions about naturally engaging on spiritual things most resonate with you, and why?

5
CREWS

WHAT

As we said earlier, in Jesus' era fishermen worked together in teams using large nets. So, when Jesus called his disciples to "fish for men" he likely had a fishing crew in mind rather than a lone fisherman casting his line. A crew is simply *a group of believers who fish together as friends for friends*. Think of the four friends who carried their paralyzed friend to Jesus in Mark 2.

WHY AND WHO

Crews mean **everyone can play**. Some of us don't have any non-Christian friends and are daunted at the prospect of going out and making them ourselves "from scratch." Others of us have loads of non-Christian friends, but need other believers in the mix if these friendships are to become evangelistically productive. Some are better at planting, others at watering, and God uses both (1 Cor. 3:6).

Similarly, crews enable us to **play to our strengths**. Some are *connectors*, good at connecting believers with unbelievers. Others are *party starters*, good at helping everyone enjoy being around each other. One may be the *carer*, good at showing care in practical ways. Another be the *intellect*, skilled at responding to objections to Christianity. Another may be the *closer*, skilled at helping someone actually step over the line of faith. And another may be the *leader*, good at coordinating and motivation crew life

HOW

Each crew should operate in a way that plays to the strengths of its members, but here are a few steps and principles that should apply to most crews.

First, someone needs to **form the crew**. Someone needs to get some *likeminded and complementary* friends together and ask them to crew together. It is best to crew with people who have natural affinity, and who have overlap in at least one of the social networks mentioned in the previous chapter. For example, parents with kids at the same school, or who live in the same neighborhood, or with a shared hobby, or at a similar life stage.

Second, update your crew on each of your **existing friendships with unbelievers**, and discuss how to help each other with these friendships. For example, if Mike shoots pool on Friday nights with work friends, maybe one or two of the guys on the crew could also start to go along and hopefully become friends with some of Mike's friends. An all-women crew I know invite unsaved friends around for dinner parties. Part of the evening is asking questions including, "What hurts at the moment?" You can imagine how deep conversations can quickly get.

Third, talk together about how you could each initiate some **new friendships with unbelievers**. For example, could two or three of you start going to the same gym together, or throw a block party together?

Fourth, remind yourselves that your strategy is **friendship**. This will shape how you operate as a crew. Don't overthink it. Just get going as friends-making-friends. Some crews may develop rhythms such as regularly eating together with your growing group of unbelieving friends. Others will be more ad hoc, but no less deliberate, in their approach.

Fifth, **fish alone then together**. An important part of crew life is encouraging one another in missional living and friend-making. Then, draw one another into those friendships.

Sixth, **meet together as a crew** to update, strategize and pray. Once every six weeks might be a good rhythm for that. Talk about how your different friendships are going, and which friends seem ripe to be invited to *read-and-discuss* or to church. Encourage one another to be sharp on their *stories* and on their *gospel communication*. Also have a comms group of some sort to keep in touch.

Seventh, keep the ultimate goal **effective fishing**. Do *not* let your crew devolve into an insular small group. Yes, you are friends, but your primary purpose is fishing together not fellowship; you will have good fellowship along the way, but eyes on the prize, people. Therefore, crews will need to evolve to suit the current "fishing season." Others may join your crew, or some crew members might need to peel off and form another crew. Some crews might only last a few months, others much longer.

Finally, it is probably best to think of "crew" as your **covert identity**, or you may unwittingly come across as sounding cliquey or weird. Think of yourselves as a fishing crew, but present yourselves as a group of friends.

REFLECTION AND DISCUSSION

What are your particular strengths in the area of friendships and evangelism?

Broadly speaking, do you need to join a crew because you have too many or too few unbelieving friends?

Who could you crew with? Next steps?

6
TOOLS

I want to focus on three simple and complementary tools you need in your friend-to-friend toolbox: *Your story*, *Read-and-discuss*, and *Gospel communication*.

YOUR STORY

Andrew said to Peter, "We have found the Messiah" (Jn. 1:41). The Samaritan woman at the well told her friends, "Come, see a man who told me everything I ever did" (Jn. 4:29 NIV). The man born blind knew little but could say, "One thing I do know. I was blind but now I see!" (Jn. 9:25 NIV). These three disciples gave testimony—or bore witness—to the power of Jesus. You also can bear witness to what Jesus has done for you. You have a story that no one can refute because it is what happened to you.

I suggest you prepare a 30-second version that captures the essence of your conversion story, and can easily be dropped into most conversations. You can also expand it to a longer version. Below are examples of 30-second conversion stories. Some are fictional and some are real stories from people I know, although I have changed the names. I find the "before, during, since" structure helpful in preparing and remembering my story, and it gives three different potential points of connection for the listener. After you read through these examples, experiment with different versions of your own story. If one of the sample stories happens to be your story, feel free to adopt it. But trust your own story.

	Before believing	**Believing**	**Since believing**
Kim	I regarded myself as something of an intellectual, and rejected Christianity based on the lack of factual evidence.	Then I came across some intelligent Christians, and I investigated the rational basis for Christianity. I was won over.	What was cerebral has now moved to my heart. I truly believe Jesus is God, and I enjoy his transforming work in my life.
Bill	I was God-aware and considered myself "spiritual," but the name of Jesus and a bloody cross were anathema to me.	A Christian friend urged me to specifically believe in Jesus, and to make him the Lord of my life. I did that.	Aligning my lifestyle with biblical ethics is still sometimes hard for me, but I am determined to follow Jesus fully.
Rob	I was a hard-working, moral guy who was better than most people. I assumed that God would accept me on the basis of my morality.	A friend of mine explained that the gospel was not a moral code to live by, but rather a gift of forgiveness to receive.	I now embrace the truth that good works are done in *response* to salvation not as a way of *gaining* salvation.
Ali	I went through a tragedy.	I realized that the tragedy didn't create my need for God, but rather revealed it.	I heeded the words of Jesus and "repented and believed in the gospel" (Mk. 1:15).

	Before believing	Believing	Since believing
Abby	I thought I was a Christian because I went to church, gave money, and read my Bible.	I heard a sermon on the Parable of the Two Sons. I realized I was the brother who had a transactional relationship with God, and really wasn't saved.	I repented not only of my sin, but also of thinking my good works saved me, and received the free gift of forgiveness and salvation.
JP	I became friends with a Christian and was drawn into her group of church friends.	After hours of discussion with one of them, I decided to become a Christian.	My biggest challenge is making Jesus Lord of every area of my life – a work in progress!
Rick	I told my Christian friend that I was not a worshiper like him. He told me I was—but that I worshiped something different than he did; money.	He explained we "worship" what we think will make us feel complete. I had to acknowledge that money would never fully satisfy me.	I now worship Jesus. I still love my job but I am not looking to that as my "feel good." I now look to Jesus for that.
Ann	I partied hard but my Christian friend never told me to change the way I behaved. I was intrigued by her non-judgmental attitude.	She asked me to do a *read-and-discuss* book with her during lunch breaks. Through that process I believed in Jesus.	Bit by bit I am feeling new. The thing I love most is knowing I am now accepted by God, even when I don't live right.

Note, you are not trying to cram in every aspect of the gospel, or even to "preach the cross." The purpose of this 30-second vignette is simply to communicate that you are a believer now and very pleased about that (1 Pet. 3:15)! Hopefully it will intrigue your listener and lead to further conversion.

READ-AND-DISCUSS

When I started to get serious about friend-to-friend, I realized I needed a resource I could use with an unbeliever (or new believer) that enabled us to talk in a structured yet relational way about what it meant to become a Christian. I needed some good, concise content around which we could have good conversation and create some momentum towards a point of decision.

To this end, I wrote a four-part booklet called *Crossing the Line of Faith*. I have personally taken about 80 people through it, and many actually crossed the line through it, and I think all the others took steps toward the line.

The first three chapters take the reader on the journey of someone who approaches the line of faith (Chapter 1), then crosses the line of faith (Chapter 2), and then starts to grow as a Christian (Chapter 3). Whether or not the reader decides to make that journey their own, it is helpful information as they consider what it means to become a Christian, and try to imagine what life would be like if they did. Then Chapter 4 contains brief answers to some of the most common objections to Christianity to hopefully enable them to give the claims and teachings of Christ a fair hearing.

When the time is right (which can be a few hours or many months into a friendship), you could say something like, "Would you be interested in reading this little booklet with me? There are only four chapters; we would each read a chapter and then meet up to discuss it over coffee." If they are already showing interest, you could preface your invitation saying something like, "I think you would find this booklet helpful for the questions you have." If they are not showing much interest, you could preface your invitation with something like, "I would love to talk you through why I am a Christian. I may have blind spots, so I would like to hear your critique, as well as to help you understand what makes me tick."

Our church uses it as a resource for a regular "Exploring Christianity" group. Digital and hard copies of *Crossing the Line of Faith* are available on Amazon.

GOSPEL COMMUNICATION

You will remember from the introductory chapter *The Glorious Gospel* that the events of the cross of Jesus form the "first" truth of the gospel; Calvary is the epicenter of the gospel message. To be saved, every unbeliever needs to come face-to-face with the stark truths of the cross such as sin, death, substitution, and resurrection. Therefore, we need to be adept at communicating the message of the cross **directly** to them.

However, some unbelievers are greatly helped by approaching the cross **less directly** at first via one of the meta-themes of the "full" gospel that I outlined in the same introductory chapter. Let us look briefly at possible direct and indirect approaches.

Direct approach to the cross

Jesus used the direct approach when he said to Martha, "I am the resurrection and the life. Whoever believes in me, though he die, yet shall he live … do you believe this?" (Jn.11:25). He also used it when he said to the stubborn pharisees, "Unless you believe that I am he you will die in yours sins" (Jn. 8:24).

Direct communication about the cross of Christ could be launched from many different verses such as John 1:12, 3:3, 3:16, 8:24, 11:25, Romans 6:3-4, 1 Corinthians 15:1-4, or 2 Corinthians 5:21. Read them through and use the one you particularly resonate with.

I tend to favor a combo of Romans 6:23 and Acts 2:38, two verses that I keep on a card in my wallet. When a friend asks me what a Christian is, or when I ask if I can tell him what a Christian is, I say something like, "Have a look at what this verse says," and I give him the card. On the card is Romans 6:23:

> For the **wages** of sin is death, but the free **gift** of God
> is eternal life **in Christ Jesus** our Lord.

I then briefly explain the bolded words:

Wage: I say something like, "Because God is holy and just, the wage/consequence of our sin is death. But in love, God sent Jesus to die in my place. God's justice against my sin fell on Jesus, not me."

Gift: Second, I say something like, "and because my sin is now no longer held against me, God kindly gives me the gift of eternal life, in heaven with him forever."

In Christ Jesus: Third, I say something like, "but notice the gift comes inside some packaging. What packaging is that?" He looks at the verse and says, "in Christ Jesus." I then take the card back, put it in my wallet and hold it out to him and say, "So if the card represents the gift of eternal life, and the wallet represents Jesus, if you want to receive the gift of eternal life, who do you need to receive into your life?" He says, "Jesus." I then say, "The verse on the other side of the card explains how to do that:

> And Peter said to them, '**Repent** and be **baptized** every one of you in the name of Jesus Christ for the **forgiveness** of your sins, and you will receive the gift of the **Holy Spirit**. (Acts 2:38)

Again, I briefly explain the bolded words saying something like, "Whenever we turn to something, we turn *from* something don't we? Turning to Jesus means turning from (repenting of) our sin, which is costly. And, getting water baptized symbolizes being washed of your sin. But wonderfully, God gives us the gift of his Holy Spirit to empower us to increasingly live in a way that pleases him." Then I say, "Would you like to turn to Jesus now, and receive him into your life? I cannot recommend it more highly."

Depending on his response, I will discuss some more and/or lead him in a prayer of salvation, or ask if he wants to read-and-discuss *Crossing The Line Of Faith* with me to properly explore what it means to become a Christian

Indirect approach

Jesus sometimes used metaphors that touched on a felt need as a way in. For example, he asked questions about *satisfaction*, talking about thirsting for water and hungering for bread (Jn. 4:13-14,

6:35). He also often used the **meta-themes** of the gospel to declare salvation. For example, in John 3 he piqued Nicodemus' interest with talk of *renewal*. To the crowds in Galilee he spoke a great deal about the *kingdom of God*, which interestingly was the basis of the thief's appeal on the cross: "Jesus, remember me when you come into your kingdom" (Lk. 23:42). To the rich young man, Jesus also housed the gospel message within the theme of the kingdom of God and the *kingdom of heaven*, calling him to store his riches in heaven (Matt. 19:16-30).

In a similar manner, how might we help our friends take some initial steps along the various avenues of gospel truth that radiate out from the cross?

We could lead with the meta-theme of **world renewal**, especially if our friend has a strong social conscience, and is passionate about caring for the poor and our planet. Or, if they are currently experiencing significant suffering, rather than hearing "your sin is so extreme that Jesus died on bloody cross" it may be better to first share how Jesus came, and will come again, to make a brand new, eternal, suffering-free heavens and earth.

We could lead with the meta-theme of the **kingdom of God** if our friend is passionate about social justice, as the gospel of the kingdom is to care for the poor and down-trodden. Or, if they are prone to latch on to "easy grace," then maybe they would be helped on their way to the cross by hearing that Jesus is King as well as Savior, and following this King requires us to give up everything else.

We could lead with the meta-theme of the **people of God** if our friend is lonely, or disappointed by selfish Western individualism.

Or, maybe they need reassurance that that they will gain a new family if they turn to Christ. Maybe they are displaced refugees – tell them of the new people they can be part of.

We could lead with the meta-theme of the returning **spirit of God** if our friend is particularly prone to anxiety. The Holy Spirit brings us peace. Or, maybe they have had a spiritual background, and need some assurance that Christianity is more than cerebral ascent to certain theological truths, that it is also a *felt* reality.

Remember, all these meta-themes are avenues to-and-from the cross. Some unbelievers go directly to the cross and get saved, and then need to walk down these various gospel avenues to enjoy the full gospel. Others need to approach the cross less directly, walking gradually toward the cross along one of these avenues. But one way of another, they need to end up at the foot of the glorious cross.

PARTING WORDS FROM AN ATHEIST CRIMINAL

Charles Peace was a convicted criminal in Victorian England. Allegedly, the prison chaplain tried to persuade him to convert shortly before he was executed, by highlighting the horrors of hell. Peace was said to respond:

> Sir, I do not share your faith. But if I did – if I believed what you say you believed – then although England were covered with broken glass from coast to coast, I would crawl the length and breadth of it on hand and knee and think the pain worthwhile,

just to save a single soul from this eternal hell of which you speak.[4]

Charles Spurgeon, the great London preacher, may have the final word:

> If sinners be damned, at least let them leap to Hell over our dead bodies. And if they perish, let them perish with our arms wrapped about their knees, imploring them to stay. If Hell must be filled, let it be filled in the teeth of our exertions, and let not one go unwarned and unprayed for.[5]

ENDNOTES

1. George McLeod, quoted in Ray Ortlund, 'Where he died, what he died for', The Gospel Coalition, April 12, 2013. www.thegospelcoalition.org/blogs/ray-ortlund/where-he-died-what-he-died-for.

2. Christopher J. H. Wright, *The Mission of God's People: A Biblical Theology of the Church's Mission* (Grand Rapids, MI: Zondervan, 2010), p. 62.

3. D. A. Carson, *The Gospel According to John* (Grand Rapids, MI: Wm. B. Eerdmans, 1991), p. 159.

4. C. H. Spurgeon, quoted in Greg Morse, 'Over Our Dead Bodies', Desiring God, January 29, 2018. www.desiringgod.org/articles/over-our-dead-bodies

5. *Ibid.*

Printed in Great Britain
by Amazon